OUTDOOR LIVING™

CAMPING

BARRY MABLETON AND JACQUELINE CHING

ROSEN
PUBLISHING

NEW YORK

Published in 2016 by The Rosen Publishing Group, Inc.
29 East 21st Street, New York, NY 10010

Library of Congress Cataloging-in-Publication Data

Mableton, Barry.
 Camping / Barry Mableton and Jacqueline Ching. -- First Edition.
     pages cm. -- (Outdoor Living)
 Includes index.
 Audience: Grades: 7-12.
 ISBN 978-1-4994-6227-2 (Library bound)
 1. Camping--Juvenile literature. 2. Family recreation--Juvenile literature. I. Ching, Jacqueline. II. Title.
 GV191.7.M25 2016
 796.54--dc23

                                                             2015016291

Manufactured in China

CONTENTS

INTRODUCTION

Have you thought about camping before but weren't sure how to plan a trip? Maybe there's a state park near your house, but you're worried about safety in the woods. Or perhaps you just can't imagine shutting down your computer and heading out into nature. Don't fret. With the right knowledge, camping can be a fun, safe, and enlightening outdoors experience!

First of all, camping is a great way to explore nature. When you're camping, you'll see wild plants and animals that you'd never catch sight of in your town or city. There are all sorts of cool critters in the woods that you won't find in your backyard. And if you know how to spot them, you can keep watch and snap some pics for your Instagram.

Another reason people go camping is to get away from day-to-day life. In the woods, you can forget about homework, tests, and updating your Facebook status. You can let all your social media hibernate while you're in the woods. Being surrounded by nature is peaceful, and it'll give your eyes a much-needed break from your phone's screen.

Camping with your family or a group of close friends can be a great way to disconnect from your routine and get in touch with nature!

Finally, camping can actually teach you some pretty essential life skills. Basic first aid, food and water preparation, and key survival skills all come with the territory when you're out in the woods. The skills you'll learn while camping are actually great reference for school tests and other emergency situations.

If you think camping may be for you, read on! We'll cover all the basics of planning a camping trip, picking the right clothes and gear, and setting up your tent. It'll be an experience you won't regret.

CHAPTER 1

MAKE A PLAN

Before any successful camping trip, the first stage is smart planning. A successful camping trip means different things to different people. For some people, camping means really roughing it. Others prefer to bring some of the comforts of home with them. Of course, camping always implies a certain amount of roughing it but to what extent depends on you. Step one, then, is to decide what you want and to make a plan.

PLANNING AND PREPARATION

Any great camping trip starts at home. This is when the important decisions must be made. What kind of food should you bring? What kind of clothes? Equipment? What about shelter?

Before deciding on these things, a good camper should decide what kind of camping experience he or she hopes to have. How

It's always a wise idea to do some research before any camping trip. Look up sites near where you live, check out where to buy camping gear, and keep an eye on the weather before any trip.

long should your trip be? Will you stay at a base camp or move to different sites? How many days will you stay at each site? How long does it take to get to each location? Do as much research as you can in advance, because you may not have great cell phone service in the woods or an opportunity to charge your cell phone or tablet.

Deciding the length of the trip is important, too. You may be content to spend a weekend away from beds, WiFi, and microwaves but not a week. Also be sure to know when the busy season is. For example, you can expect a crowd in the Great Smoky Mountains National Park during the peak of autumn colors. If you are traveling with friends, discuss everyone's expectations beforehand.

Campers who expect relaxation and contemplation may not mix well with campers intent on breaking hiking records. Make time for everyone to explore on his or her own.

For your first few trips, practice your camping skills closer to home and in well-traveled areas. It takes years to become an expert who knows by instinct how to keep safe in the wilderness.

An important part of your plan is weather. You can start by choosing a season when your tent is least likely to be flooded by rain, but you should also keep track of weather systems immediately before your trip. Check the forecast online for the full duration of your trip. Always be prepared for the unexpected.

Many weather apps can give you live updates about changing weather. But be sure to contact your campsite in advance and check on the strength of cell signals before relying on your smartphone.

Finally, plan a budget. How much money do you intend to spend? If money is tight, don't go too far into the wilderness. The farther out you go, the more specialized your equipment will need to be. Remember, the longer your trip is, the more supplies you'll have to bring. Ask about camping fees at your destination. And don't forget to factor in travel costs such as gas and parking fees.

PICKING THE RIGHT CAMPGROUND

There are over sixty thousand camp and park facilities in the United States—and each one is unique! The terrain in a coastal area will differ greatly from an alpine highland. You will need to do some research before choosing a site.

Be aware of the campground's geography and native plants and animals. Find out in advance if your camp is near a body of water, thickly forested, or steep and mountainous. Your research should also help you stay far away from thick woods, deep grass, and stagnant ponds; these places strongly attract insects. It is always easier to camp at established campgrounds. Most of them have basic amenities, such as safe water supplies, showers, and bathrooms.

ACTIVITIES

Another factor in choosing a campground is the activities it offers. Is there fishing? Canoeing? Kayaking? Hiking? Climbing? Remember that for certain activities you will need special equipment and supplies, such as a fishing rod. You may also need special licenses.

PLANNING YOUR CAMPING TRIP ONLINE

A great resource ahead of any camping trip is the government website Recreation.gov. This one-stop site coordinates camping information, trip planning, and reservations for twelve different US agencies, including the National Park Service (NPS) and the Forest Service. Advance reservations are available for over twenty-five hundred federal areas and over sixty

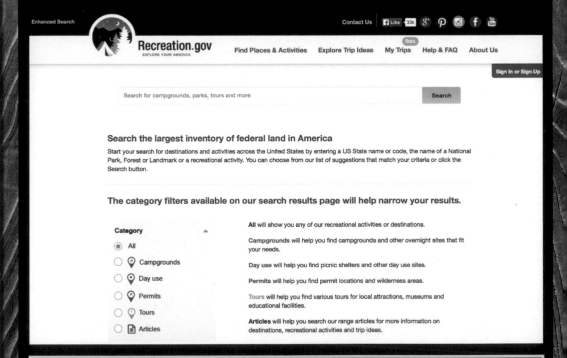

Online resources, such as the website Recreation.gov, can help potential campers find suitable campsites in their area. You can even reserve lodging for many parks in advance online!

thousand facilities and activities. These activities include camping, hiking, mountain climbing, canoeing, and more.

Before booking your reservation, be sure to contact park officials at your planned destination. Call or send an e-mail so they can inform you about unseasonable weather, bear warnings, availability of campsites, additional fees, available activities, rules, and regulations.

PERMITS

Camping permits help park officials keep track of the number of visitors, in case of emergency, and to control the use of park facilities. As soon as you choose a destination, apply for the necessary permits. You may be able to get a permit when you arrive, you may need one in advance, or you may not need one at all. Rules differ from place to place.

IMPROVISE, TOO!

While it's always smart to do your research, not everything can be planned out. You may not have a choice where you camp. The weather may change drastically. Some of your experience will depend on luck; it will also depend on your attitude and creativity. You're on an adventure, and the most important thing you can bring with you is your ability to improvise.

CHAPTER 2

LAYER UP: PACKING CLOTHING

For any camping trip, the essential rule is to pack smart. Make a complete list of everything you'll need—including clothes. Proper clothing is one of the essentials. You'll want to pack clothes that aren't too bulky or too heavy to carry. Specialized outdoor wear is available at outdoor suppliers, but before you buy a whole new wardrobe, check your closet first.

USE COMMON SENSE

The basic question when packing for a camping trip is, "What will the weather be?" Does the forecast predict rain, heat, or frost? Pack accordingly. Of course, no weather forecast is 100 percent accurate, and any camper could get caught in unexpected showers or

An important rule of packing for a camping trip is to remember that whatever you pack you'll have to carry. Be wise and bring only the essentials. Everything should fit in a backpack.

a heat wave. Temperatures at some campsites can range quite a bit from morning to night—especially in the desert. Make sure you're prepared for changes in weather.

If you plan on being outdoors for a long time, then the expense of buying outdoor wear makes sense. However, if you're a beginning camper, stick with the versatile classics. In mild weather, clothes made of cotton such as T-shirts and jeans work well. They are comfortable and lightweight. You can also layer several T-shirts as needed. However, because cotton absorbs moisture, it doesn't work in wet or cold weather. Therefore, most outdoor clothing is made from synthetic fabrics.

Sweats are useful, too. You can sleep in them, and they're very warm. If possible, choose sweats that are 50 percent acrylic.

THE CAMPER'S GUIDE TO LAYERING

Since there are no guarantees when it comes to weather, the all-purpose solution is to layer your clothes. Layering gives you maximum flexibility.

For the inner layer, choose wool or synthetic fabrics. Long underwear made of polyester or polypropylene may be your best bet. It keeps moisture away from the body. In summer, it keeps you cool and dry even when you sweat, and in winter it provides added insulation.

The middle layer should insulate you. Choose a fleece jacket or wool sweater. Fleece is lighter and absorbs less moisture than wool.

The outer layer protects against weather. Choose a waterproof windbreaker. This inexpensive item is lightweight and warm and can also protect you from rain. In the mountains, weather is even more unpredictable. Rainwear will be needed. Wet skin and clothing, plus low temperatures and wind, can lead to hypothermia, a serious illness caused by prolonged exposure to cold.

They cost less, weigh less, and dry more quickly than 100 percent cotton clothing.

Because of the increasing popularity of outdoor activities, there are more choices in outerwear than ever. Today's parkas and jackets combine natural and synthetic fabrics and offer warmth without additional weight or bulk, which makes them easier to carry. A down vest is another useful item of clothing. People allergic to down can find synthetic alternatives. In winter, bring a parka or a jacket. In summer, pack your shorts. And, of course, in any season, don't forget a supply of clean socks and underwear.

When you are exposed to the elements, the key to keeping warm is to conserve your body's heat. You may have heard the bit of old wisdom: "If your feet are cold, put on a hat." This is because you lose a lot of body heat from your head. Hats come in wool, fleece, or acrylic. Don't leave your hat at home!

PROTECT YOUR FEET

Any camping trip is sure to involve a good deal of walking. You may need to hike to reach the best vistas. Therefore, you can do yourself a big favor by investing in good socks. They stand between you and pain. Socks made for walking and hiking come in natural and synthetic blends. They give your feet support, protect your tendons, and absorb shock. They also keep your feet warm or cool and, above all, dry.

Even more important than good socks is a good pair of shoes. If you are only planning short hikes on gentle trails, a good running shoe will be just fine. (Think of what you would wear to the gym or in a P.E. class.) Whatever pair you pick, make sure to wear shoes that give plenty of support and absorb a lot of shock. In warmer weather, or if you are planning water activities, it's a good idea to bring waterproof sandals.

Investing in a good pair of hiking boots is a smart idea for anybody planning on taking long hikes while camping. They'll keep your feet safe and comfortable over rough terrain.

Hiking boots are preferable for longer hikes because they are sturdier, give you ankle support, and absorb shock. A good pair of hiking boots can last you for many camping trips, so invest in a good pair. When you go shopping for boots, make sure they fit properly. Also, it's smart to bring the socks you plan to use while hiking and try the boots on with the socks. Walk down an incline and see if your heel stays in place. There should be no slippage when you are hiking downhill in your boots.

CHAPTER 3

PACK SMART: CAMPING GEAR

Any camper knows that the woods can be rough. It may be hard to sleep or uncomfortable in your sleeping bag. Temperatures may vary, and without the right gear, you may not be best prepared for everything that comes your way. With limited space (after all, you'll have to carry most of what you pack), picking the right gear is crucial. A solid backpack, the right tent, and a cozy sleeping bag will make all the difference on any camping excursion.

CARRY IT ON YOUR BACK

When camping, your backpack becomes your portable home. It carries everything you need. Make sure everything fits in the backpack and that the pack fits well on you.

Cheaper backpacks come one-size-fits-all. They are usually adequate for short trips. If you spend more money, you can get one

When a camper heads out into the wild, his or her backpack must carry everything. A smart camper will pack only the essentials and buy a sturdy backpack that can handle the weight.

that has adjustable straps. Invest in a good hip belt. It can take some of the pressure off your neck and shoulders.

There are two basic types of backpack: external frame and internal frame. External frame backpacks have an aluminum or nylon metal frame attached to the outside of the pack to support it. These packs are great for general backpacking, especially for heavy loads. A good external frame backpack usually costs between 100 and 200 dollars. Cheaper ones exist, but beware of cheaply designed frames that may come apart under a heavy load.

Internal frame backpacks are less bulky and give you more freedom of movement. Mountaineers, skiers, and climbers prefer this pack because it tends to balance more easily. The downside is this snugly fitting pack will leave a hiker perspiring in warm temperatures.

Daypacks are smaller than backpacks. As with full-size backpacks, the key to choosing a good daypack is support. Look for a curve on the back of the pack matching the curve of your spine. Again, choose one with a good hip belt.

Daypacks come with a variety of features. You will probably find it useful to have a couple of outside pockets (for pocketknives, water bottles, and snacks) and maybe an ax loop, on which to hang additional items.

CHOOSING THE RIGHT TENT

A tent is a big purchase, but the right one can last you a lifetime. It's also essential if you want to get a good night's sleep.

The prices of tents vary widely. The major differences between different types of tents are the materials and the stitching. More expensive tents are double stitched, which is rather labor intensive. Some tents are also waterproof, but others are merely water resistant. When it comes to poles, aluminum alloy poles are considered the best in terms of weight and durability.

Tents are designed for different camping conditions and seasons. A summer tent is light and lets in a lot of air. It may have mesh windows and a mesh roof for viewing the night sky and keeping out mosquitoes. A three-season tent makes sense if you plan on doing a lot of camping. It works well in mild weather but can also handle heavy rainstorms. An all-season tent gives extra protection against

Dome tents, such as the one shown here, give lots of space but can be heavy to carry. Different types of tents are suited for different camping excursions. Which tent is right for you?

sharp winds, snow, or sleet. It also weighs two to four pounds (one to two kilograms) more than the others. If you expect to do a lot of backpacking or hiking, you may decide to sacrifice comfort for weight. Generally, the tougher tents will weigh more.

In addition to a good tent, a tarp is another useful—but optional—item. Tarps provide shade on hot days and a roof when it rains. Tarps can also protect firewood you've collected from rain and moisture. Some tarps come with poles; others are held up by ropes tied to trees. Unless you want your tarp to become a basin of water when it rains, you have to elevate its center. Usually this can be done with an aluminum center pole or by hanging the tarp over a taut rope so rainwater runs off.

TENT SHAPES CHECKLIST

Different tent shapes have different pros and cons. Read this list to decide which tent is best for your camping adventure.

SHAPE	PROS	CONS
A-Frame Tent	Tent will withstand wind and rain. Simple design.	Cramped interior. Some require stakes; others are freestanding.
Dome Tent	Good three-season tent. Upright walls leave lots of room.	Heavy to carry. May blow away if not properly staked.
Hoop Tent	Light and easy to set up. High ceilings.	Not durable in heavy winds or storms.
Pyramid Tent	Light and easy to set up.	No built-in floor means no protection from water or bugs.

SELECTING YOUR SLEEPING BAG

Camping almost inevitably involves sleeping outdoors. There's no way around it. This means the most important item to bring is a sleeping bag. When buying a sleeping bag, ask yourself how much you think you'll go camping. If you camp a lot, invest in a higher-quality bag. In general, a three-season bag is the best buy. A good rule of thumb is to think of the coldest temperatures you will be sleeping in. You can always leave your bag unzipped if it gets too hot, but there's not much you can do if it gets too cold.

You can choose your sleeping bag based on its temperature or comfort rating. A summer fair-weather bag has a minimum rating of between 40 and 50 degrees Fahrenheit (4 and 10 degrees Celsius). This means it will keep you snug when it's 40 to 50 degrees Fahrenheit (4 to 10 degrees Celsius) outside. For cooler weather, choose one that has a minimum rating of between 20 and 25 degrees Fahrenheit (-7 and -4 degrees Celsius) or, for winter camping, a minimum rating of 10 degrees Fahrenheit (-12 degrees Celsius) or lower. Keep in mind, however, that the manufacturers rate their own products and there is no universal rating system for bags.

Sleeping bags are filled with either down or synthetic materials. There are pros and cons to both. Down bags are light, warm, and compressible. Goose down is the best insulator. However, a good down bag can be very expensive. Also, if your bag should get wet, a synthetic bag will keep you warmer than a down bag.

Synthetic bags have improved greatly and are usually far cheaper than down bags. In weight and compression, however, they still can't beat down bags. A down bag can weigh 3 pounds (1.4 kilograms), whereas a synthetic bag with the same insulating power weighs 2 or 3 pounds (1 to 1.4 kg) more. Down bags compress about 25 percent smaller, too. If you do choose a synthetic bag, don't pack it up tightly. Doing so can make the fibers break down and your bag lose its insulation.

Sleeping outdoors can be rough and chilly. But having the right sleeping bag for the season will keep a camper warm, rested, and cozy.

SLEEPING PADS

Traditionally, Native Americans and pioneers laid down pine needles, grass, dry leaves, or straw for bedding. A more practical choice is available to today's campers: the sleeping pad. With such a pad, the rocks or roots underneath you won't be as noticeable. The sleeping pad will also keep you warmer.

You can buy foam pads or air mattresses to use as sleeping pads, but old sleeping bags or extra blankets will do the trick, too. As always, you have to factor in bulkiness and weight when packing these extra items.

Another consideration when choosing a sleeping bag is its size and shape. You'll want enough room to stretch out but not too much room for air. Your body has to heat that extra space. Before buying a sleeping bag, try it on for size. Roll around in it and feel the fit. The basic shapes are mummy (a tight-fitting bag with a hood), semi-mummy (like the mummy but with a looser fit), and rectangular (open at the top and, thus, less heat-efficient).

Lastly, check the zipper before you buy your sleeping bag. Compare the zipper quality of several bags.

OTHER BASIC GEAR

Remember that in the woods, you won't have plumbing but you will still need to keep clean. Don't forget basic toiletries:

toothbrush and toothpaste, towels, lip balm and sunscreen, wet wipes, and toilet paper. There may be other things you will need, such as sanitary napkins or tampons.

You also won't want to be without a flashlight. Many campers prefer a miner's light, which is worn on the head, to free up their hands for other tasks. Remember to bring extra batteries.

You also won't want to go hungry. It takes a lot of skill to build a fire without a lighter or matches, so make sure to bring plenty. Keep waterproof matches in a waterproof container. A butane lighter dries easily and lights repeatedly.

A knife always comes in handy for cooking, setting up tents and tarps, and emergencies. In addition to a sturdy knife, you may want to pack a multiuse camp tool.

Finally, don't forget a compass and a map. If you get lost in the woods, these tools can help you find your way back home. Overall, the guiding principle is to pack wisely! Each extra item brought is another pound or two to carry.

CHAPTER 4

SETTING UP CAMP

The next step in an expert camping experience is setting up camp. Of course, finding the right spot is essential. If you plan to camp during peak season, you must plan ahead. In summer, don't expect to camp at popular destinations, such as Yellowstone or Yosemite, without reserving a campsite. Many campgrounds also have sites available on a first-come, first-served basis. Use Recreation.gov to make reservations and learn other important info about campsites.

At any park, make the visitor center your first stop. There you will find information on attractions, facilities, and activities. Some parks offer scenic drives, historic tours, cruises, and ranger-guided programs. The park staff will also answer questions about accommodations, services, and special attractions.

FINDING THE RIGHT CAMPSITE

At your destination, park officials may direct you to where you are allowed to camp. However, you still must pick a site to pitch your tent and build a fire. You should pick a place where there is an existing fire ring or fire pit. This will minimize your impact on the environment.

Take advantage of daylight to check around your campsite for dangerous ditches, poison ivy or poison oak, beehives, and anything else that could lead to an unfortunate encounter in the dark.

Many parks have designated areas as campgrounds. Usually, there will be better facilities available near campgrounds. Check beforehand if a reservation or deposit is needed.

VISITOR CENTER
OPEN ➡

CAMPGROUND
200 YARDS ➡

DAY USE FEES
·PARKING
(SENIORS $3.00) $5.00

DOGS ALLOWED ON PAVED AREAS & LIVE OAK TRAIL ONLY

OVERNIGHT FEES
·CAMPSITE (SENIORS $ 5.00) $12.00
·ADDITIONAL MOTOR VEHICLE $5.00
·Backpackers (No Dogs) PER PERSON $3.00
BACKPACKERS REGISTER AT VISITOR CENTER PER PERSON

GUIDELINES FOR THE PERFECT CAMPSITE

Follow these rules when searching for your campsite:
- Don't camp under dead trees, whose branches could fall.
- Don't camp near gullies, overhanging rocks, and bear trails.
- Don't camp under a lone tree, in case of a lightning storm. Stick to higher ground and avoid areas that turn into swamps after rain.
- Find good exposure. You'll want sun in the morning for warmth and shade in the afternoon.
- Make sure there's plenty of firewood nearby.
- Camp away from game trails so you don't disturb animals.

Before pitching your tent, choose a level place and clear away all debris. You'll sleep better with fewer rocks and twigs under the tent. Pitch your tent away from the fire. Don't pitch your tent on ground foliage. You have your sleeping pad for comfort and warmth.

BUILDING A CAMPFIRE

You don't want to be responsible for burning down the forest. Follow fire-building safety guidelines and be proactive in protecting the environment. You can start by making a small fire so that you burn only the wood you need. Don't burn live wood. Besides, collecting fallen branches is part of the fun.

Although fire regulations are often posted in campgrounds or at trailheads, you should always ask park officials about current conditions. In the summer or in a drought, open fires are prohibited, but you will still be able to use your pack stove or a pit fireplace, which can be found in certain campgrounds. You may be required to have a shovel and a bucket of water near the fire. Sometimes you need a fire permit.

You can get up-to-date information by calling any local office of the US Forest Service or National Park Service. It's important to learn the regulations before you strike that match.

STEPS TO SAFELY BUILD A FIRE

Make sure your fire ring sits about six feet (two meters) clear of any flammable materials, such as dried twigs, grass, or overhanging branches. There should be a circle of rocks around the ring to keep the wind from blowing out your fire.

Make sure to gather enough firewood first. You will need small, dry twigs, as well as larger sticks of wood. Build a tent-shaped structure in the middle of the fire ring. Take your butane lighter or matches and light the small twigs. As they catch, start to feed larger sticks to the flames.

If you are cooking with coals, you should dig a trench near the fire circle to store the coals. From the trench, you can easily shovel the coals into the fire.

A bonfire can be fun, keep a campsite warm, and serve as a grill to heat food, but remember fire safety and try to use existing fire pits at your campgrounds.

FOOD FOR THE OUTDOORS

Being outdoors takes a lot of energy. Carrying a thirty-pound (fourteen-kilogram) pack over long trails can really build up an appetite. A good rule of thumb is to carry two pounds (one kilogram) of food (excluding packaging) per day per person. Look for food that will keep your energy up and that is lightweight, easy to prepare, and won't spoil easily. Make sure any perishable food, such as milk, butter, and mayonnaise, is kept cool to stay fresh.

A great idea is to plan all your cooked meals in advance. Measure all the ingredients and place them into separate bags. Prepare some fresh vegetables (for example, carrots and celery) in bags, too. Hearty foods such as peanut butter sandwiches or dried salami are perfect for camping. You can indulge in eggs and bacon for breakfast. You'll need lots of calories to enjoy outdoor activities. Don't skimp on proteins or fat, the body's fuel. Also, bring along lots of snacks. Nuts are high in energy. Fresh fruit such as apples and oranges are another great snack, although they can get heavy if you bring too many. Don't forget trail mix and granola bars.

For longer trips, freeze-dried food is the most practical in terms of weight and ease of preparation. It also offers variety, from macaroni and cheese to noodle and rice dishes. On the other hand, freeze-dried food requires water. One meal might require two and a half cups (half a liter) of boiling water to cook. Consider your water sources before packing. You can supplement freeze-dried foods with crackers, cereals, and dried soups.

If you are planning to cook, don't forget to pack utensils and cooking staples, such as oil, flour, and butter. Minimally, you'll need a pot (for soups, hot drinks, and treating water), a frying pan, fire grill, cooking spoon, spatula, can opener, pot holders, cutlery, and dishes.

WAYS TO TREAT WATER

The water around organized campgrounds is usually treated to be safe, but that's not true in the wilderness. Unfortunately, most natural water sources today contain either biological or chemical contaminants. The simple rule is: Don't drink untreated water unless it's an emergency.

This warning is a very serious one. Untreated water may contain such bacteria as *E. coli*, *Salmonella*, and *Vibrio cholerae*. Bacteria, viruses, and parasites can leave you with diarrhea, vomiting, or worse. These biological contaminants can also cause typhoid, strep throat, dysentery, and other diseases. Fortunately, there are a few ways to treat water that make it safe to drink.

TREATING WATER WITH IODINE

Iodine, if used correctly, will kill most waterborne organisms. It comes in tablet, crystal, and liquid form. Iodine is even effective against *Giardia*, a parasite that causes stomach cramps, diarrhea, and vomiting. In order for iodine to kill *Giardia*, the water has to be at least 69 degrees Fahrenheit (21 degrees Celsius).

After adding iodine, wait at least thirty minutes before drinking the water. For better-tasting water, add neutralizing tablets and shake the water. Drink mixes will also cover the taste of the iodine.

TREATING WATER BY BOILING

Bringing water to a boil can kill all parasites and bacteria. To be safe, boil water for three to five minutes.

TREATING WATER BY FILTRATION

Portable lightweight water filters will strain out most bacteria, viruses, and parasites. Water filters can weigh as little as one pound (half a kilogram) but can be fairly expensive. Remember to bring an extra filter for trips longer than one night.

None of these methods is 100 percent effective, so you may want to combine two of them to be safe. For example, iodine alone is ineffective against the parasite *Crypto-sporidium*, which produces fever, vomiting, fatigue, and diarrhea. Water filters alone cannot strain away the tiniest of organisms. These need to be killed by boiling the water or by adding iodine. Some water filters have built-in iodine chambers to guarantee full protection. However you choose to treat your water, avoid possible animal contamination by going upstream

Boiling water is one of the simplest ways to kill bacteria and parasites. Be certain to keep water boiling for three to five minutes to make sure it is safe to drink.

from where you find evidence of animals, such as a beaver dam, to draw your water. Following these tips and combining different techniques will give you the best shot at safe drinking water.

CHAPTER 5

ENCOUNTERING WILDLIFE

Camping isn't all about exercise and perfecting your outdoors survival skills. It's also an excellent way to come into contact with wild plants and animals. While exploring the outdoors, keep your distance from any wild animals and don't provoke them. By following basic trail etiquette, you can protect yourself from danger.

Although it's safer to explore the wild as a group rather than alone, keep your group small. That will make it easier to avoid disturbing animals and plants. If there is a trail, stick to it. If you need to go off the trail, step gently around delicate turf.

Singing or whistling as you walk along a trail warns animals of your approach and prevents them from being startled. Most bears, for instance, will go away when they detect your presence. When it comes to wild animals, simply stay out of their way. They are usually more afraid of you than you are of them.

Binoculars are a great way to observe animals from a distance. Not only do they make it easier to see birds and other wildlife, but they ensure campers don't disturb an animal's environment.

Although viewing wildlife is an exciting part of camping, it should be done from a safe distance. Use binoculars or a camera with a lens that can zoom. You are more likely to spot wildlife if you walk slowly and stop occasionally to look around. Research any specific animals you want to see in advance on the Internet, and bring a field guide when you camp. The more you know about wildlife, the better you can protect it and yourself from mutual harm.

BIG, BAD BEARS

There are about 625,000 bears in North America. In the wilderness, bears tend to keep their distance. In US national parks, however, bears are more accustomed to human company and may be bolder. Don't ever feed a bear, especially if it is a cub. You may provoke its mother's anger.

Don't give a bear reason to rob your camp. Odors—even the ones coming from your cooler—attract bears. Keep your food and cooking items locked up tightly or stored high in a tree sling. Make sure your food is at least eight feet (two meters) off the ground and four feet (one meter) away from the nearest weight-bearing branch. Never keep food in your tent. In the dark, when bears are most active, use a flashlight to warn them of your presence.

Black bears outnumber grizzly bears, which are an endangered species. However, you are just as likely to encounter a grizzly as a black bear, because grizzlies are more aggressive. Most bears attack when they are startled. If you should have such an encounter, back up slowly (never run) while singing or talking. Don't be threatening and always give the bear an escape route. Avoid eye contact.

If you are charged by a bear, remember that playing dead works with a grizzly but not with a black bear. If a black bear charges you, shout and kick. If you climb up a tree, make sure you can get higher than twelve feet (four meters). Small grizzlies and black bears can climb trees, too.

If you see bear warnings posted on trails, contact park staff for details. It means that bear activity is greater than normal, and you may have to take extra precautions by avoiding natural bear foods such as berries, nuts, fish, and animal flesh.

SLITHERING SNAKES

Most people don't take precautions against snakebites very seriously. However, it's important to be very careful when outdoors, particularly if you're camping somewhere with a large snake population or native, venomous snakes. In snake country, never reach into a hole or bush where your vision is obscured. Never sit down without inspecting the area around you. Many snakes are

While many snakes are harmless, certain snakes can be dangerous and will attack if provoked. Be mindful of bushes and holes, and slowly move away from any snake you spot.

camouflaged, meaning they blend in. Be careful when stepping over logs. Walk slowly so as not to startle a snake, and avoid walking at night, when snakes are most active.

BUSY BUGS

The woods are prime tick territory, and places near water are great for mosquitoes. There are also gnats, ants, yellow jackets, wasps, and a host of other insects to worry about in the outdoors. So, unless you're camping in the winter, pack protection.

Mainstream insect repellents use DEET, which is effective at repelling insects but toxic in large quantities to humans. Use it sparingly and keep it away from hands, eyes, mouth, and open wounds. Read product labels. A 30 percent DEET concentration is enough to do the job. There are alternatives to using a DEET product, but their effectiveness may vary. You can also use natural insect repellent products, mosquito coils, and citronella candles.

TREATING DIFFERENT ANIMAL BITES

If someone is bitten by a bear or other wild mammal, try to stop any heavy bleeding with bandages and pressure. If there is no bleeding, wash the wound thoroughly with water and soap. Apply a clean dressing to the wound. Treat the victim for shock. Get medical help as soon as possible to prevent infection. If your phone has service, call 911. Symptoms of infection are pain and tenderness, redness, heat, swelling, pus, and red streaks around the wound. Try to identify the specific animal that bit the person.

If bitten by a snake, the best thing to do is to get professional medical help as soon as possible. Wash the wound and immobilize the injured area, keeping it lower than the heart, if possible. Take an antihistamine to control the reaction to the venom. Keep very still or walk very slowly to keep your pulse down and to slow your blood flow.

Contrary to popular belief, you should not apply ice, cut the wound, or use a tourniquet on a snakebite. Encourage bleeding from the wound and try suctioning it. Using your mouth to suction should always be your last resort. If possible, note the snake's markings to help identify it when medical help arrives.

If you are stung by an insect, try to kill it so you can identify it. Ice is a popular home remedy for insect bites. Many insect bites are harmless, but they can be life threatening for those who have a severe allergy to the venom. The most common insect-bite allergy is to the bee sting. If a bee stings you, remove the stinger as quickly as possible.

If the victim is allergic to bees, and particularly if he or she has been stung a number of times, seek medical help immediately. Symptoms of an allergic reaction include swelling of the throat, dizziness, redness or discoloration around the bite, itching, hives, and difficulty breathing.

You can also try spraying your clothes with the DEET product before spraying yourself. Be sure to thoroughly wash any clothes sprayed with a product containing DEET later. You can also spray your tent, but make sure you let it air out and be careful not to spray any food supplies.

Expert campers are more wary of ticks than anything else. Tick bites can easily get infected and, even worse, can cause Lyme disease. To avoid ticks, take the precaution of wearing long pants and high socks, especially in springtime. Spray insect repellent on your legs, too. It's also a good idea to check your legs for ticks every hour or two if you're walking through bushes.

POISONOUS PLANTS

The most important rule to remember about plants in the wild is to never eat anything. Any plants you can't identify could be poisonous. This includes its leaves, berries, stems, mushrooms, and all other plant parts. Some poisonous plants closely resemble other, safe plants. If in any doubt at all, don't eat it.

Coming into contact with poison ivy will result in a nasty itch that lasts up to two weeks. Identify the plant by its leaves, which grow in groups of three, as seen above.

Learn to recognize poison ivy, poison sumac, and poison oak. These are the most common poisonous plants you'll see when camping. Coming into contact with them causes an allergic reaction on the skin that results in itchy red rashes and sometimes blisters. Luckily, the rash is not contagious and goes away within two weeks. Scratching will spread infection.

If you come into contact with any of these poisonous plants, wash the area thoroughly with strong soap, then apply calamine lotion. Running hot water on it can alleviate the itching. Remove and thoroughly wash any clothing that may have come into contact with the plant oils.

CHAPTER 6

WHAT TO DO IN AN EMERGENCY

The absolute best way to prepare for any emergency that may happen while camping is to take a basic course in first aid. It only takes a few hours and could really save a life. Many organizations offer basic first aid courses. The American Red Cross recommends its course Responding to Emergencies for campers. The course covers severe bleeding, internal bleeding, shock, muscle and skeletal injuries, diagnoses of illness, how to move victims, and what to do if help can't reach you. Participants are certified in both first aid and basic CPR. Call your local American Red Cross for more information. First aid is important for anyone to know, but especially for campers.

Before leaving on a camping trip, give trusted friends and family members your itinerary. Include details on where you're camping as well as contact information for both the campground office and the nearest forest service office.

Know that conditions differ from one campground to another. Although you may have camped before, don't take things for granted. Aside from bears, snakes, poison ivy, and polluted water, the terrain itself can pose a hazard. Avoid taking unnecessary risks, such as walking on loose rocks and mud near slopes and cliffs, standing under dead trees and dead branches in a storm, and moving quickly through heavy brush. It is also a good idea to familiarize yourself with the terrain around your campsite before nightfall, taking note of any holes, ditches, or other potential hazards. In other words, pay attention to any new environment.

SHOCK

Shock is the failure of the cardiovascular system to keep enough blood circulating to the heart, lungs, and brain. Many injuries, infections, and illnesses can cause shock. Sometimes shock is the result of a severe allergic reaction. It is life threatening if left untreated.

Immediately after an injury, observe the victim for symptoms of shock. These include confusion; very fast or very slow pulse rate; very fast or very slow breathing; shivering and weakness in the arms or legs; cool and moist skin; pale or bluish skin, lips, and fingernails; and enlarged pupils.

BLEEDING

If someone is bleeding heavily, take first aid measures to stop the bleeding, prevent infection, and prevent shock.

FIRST AID MEASURES TO FIGHT SHOCK

If you anticipate that shock may follow an injury, take these first aid measures:

- Maintain the victim's body temperature. If the victim is cold, wrap him or her in a blanket. If hot, keep him or her cool.
- Keep the victim lying down, comfortable, and calm. This improves circulation.
- If the victim is not suspected of having head, neck, or back injuries or leg fractures, elevate the legs.
- If you suspect head or neck injuries, keep the victim lying flat. If vomiting occurs, turn the victim on his or her side.
- If the victim has trouble breathing, move him or her into a semi-reclining position.

To control bleeding, apply direct pressure to the wound. Use a dressing, if available. Otherwise, a towel or piece of clothing will do. If the dressing becomes soaked with blood, always apply new dressings over old ones, so as not to disturb the wound.

After dressing the wound, elevate the wound above the level of the heart and continue to apply direct pressure (unless you suspect there is a fracture).

Apply a bandage over the wound. Pressure should be used in applying the bandage. However, be sure to check the pulse to make

If any scrapes or falls result in heavy bleeding, use direct pressure and a bandage to stop the bleeding.

sure the bandage is not cutting off circulation. A slow pulse rate or bluish fingertips or toes may be signs that the bandage is too tight.

TREATING BURNS

Burns are most severe when located on the face, neck, hands, feet, and genitals or spread over large parts of the body. Burns cause pain, infection, and shock.

First-degree burns are the least severe type of burn. First-degree burns usually exhibit redness or discoloration, mild swelling, and pain. Sunburns are the most common type of first-degree burn. For treatment, soak the burn in or run it under cool water. Then apply moist dressings and bandage loosely.

Second-degree burns may be the most painful because although the burn is deeper, the nerve endings are still intact. With severe burns, don't break any blisters. Apply first aid ointment and dry dressings, then bandage loosely. Treat the victim for shock and get medical help as soon as possible. Do not use ice or water, as these may increase the risk of shock. In a third-degree burn, damage extends to all layers of the skin. Third-degree burns or worse require immediate medical treatment.

DEFEAT DEHYDRATION & HEATSTROKE

Dehydration occurs quickly, especially during strenuous activity at higher altitudes. Always carry at least a full bottle of consumable water. Remember that water may not be readily available at your campsite. If you need to treat water from a natural spring, be sure to do so in sufficient quantities to stay hydrated.

Vomiting and diarrhea are not life threatening until they cause dehydration. Even if someone has a problem taking in food and liquid, it is important that he or she take frequent sips of water to replace any lost fluids. In cases of severe dehydration, get medical help as soon as possible.

In extreme heat, heatstroke can also occur. Heatstroke is caused by a combination of high temperatures, sun, and strenuous exercise. Take immediate action. When a person has heatstroke, his or her body temperature rises so high that brain damage and death can result unless the body is cooled quickly.

Symptoms of heatstroke include hot, red, and dry skin; small pupils; and very high body temperature. If you observe any of these symptoms, cool the victim as soon as possible, in any way possible. This means moving the person to a cool, shaded place; using a fan; applying a cool body wash with a sponge or wet towel; or putting

Dehydration is all too common when you're hiking or engaged in other physical activity outdoors without drinking enough water. Always carry enough clean drinking water to keep hydrated.

him or her in a tub of cool water. Treat the person for shock. Do not give the person anything by mouth, and get medical help as soon as possible.

HYPOTHERMIA

The counterpart to heatstroke is hypothermia. Exposure to the severe cold, high winds, and dampness can cause this life-threatening condition. Look for symptoms such as shivering, dizziness, numbness, confusion, weakness, impaired judgment, impaired vision, and drowsiness. In its advanced stages, the victim

FIRST AID KIT: DON'T LEAVE HOME WITHOUT IT

Before camping, you should purchase a first aid kit. It is not enough to pack a kit; you need to familiarize yourself with its contents and learn what to do in an emergency. The American Red Cross provides a list of the basic contents of a first aid kit and how to use them on its website. If you already own a first aid kit, check it periodically to restock items that have been used and to replace expired medications.

A basic first aid kit is easy to purchase and essential to have on hand. It will contain the most critical tools to have on hand in the event of any camping injury.

will experience a loss of consciousness and decreased pulse and breathing rates, which can be fatal.

For treatment, keep the victim warm and dry. Move him or her to a shelter and remove any wet clothing. Use sleeping bags and emergency blankets to make sure the person is well insulated from the ground as well as from the wind. If the victim is fully conscious, give him or her warm liquids. Get medical help as soon as possible.

FRACTURES AND SPRAINS

Symptoms of fractures and sprains include pain, tenderness, swelling, bruising, a feeling of bones rubbing together, and an inability to move the injured body part. Follow these quick steps to treat fractures and sprains:

- Control bleeding, if necessary.
- Tie splints to the affected area to prevent further movement, taking care not to cause additional pain to the victim.
- Apply a cold compress to reduce pain and swelling. Treat the victim for shock.
- Get medical help as soon as possible.

WHAT TO DO IF YOU GET LOST

Although no one plans on getting lost, you should create an action plan in case it happens. First, if you decide to go hiking alone, make sure to tell others where you're going and when you'll be back. Second, there are some light items you should carry: waterproof matches, a fire starter, a multiuse camp tool, a whistle, a compass, and an emergency blanket. More important, bring a full water bottle and an extra supply of granola bars.

If you think you're lost, don't panic. Others know the direction you were headed in and will start looking for you. Look around to see if anything—such as an unusual tree or a mountain peak—looks familiar or if there are tracks you can follow. If nothing looks familiar or if it's getting dark, stay put and let others find you. Try to stay warm and spread out your food and water supplies. If you have your matches and fire starter, build a safe fire. If you hear someone, use your whistle to signal your location. Three short blasts is the universal distress call.

CHAPTER 7

CAMP GREEN! ECO-FRIENDLY CAMPING

Camping goes beyond simply interacting with nature. Any responsible camper also has a responsibility to leave his or her campsite in better condition than he or she found it. Campgrounds see countless visitors each year, but if each camper does his or her share, then we can minimize our impact on nature.

WHERE'S THE BATHROOM?

If your campground doesn't have toilet facilities, ask park officials about waste disposal. Aside from its obvious offensiveness, human waste presents a serious health hazard. It contains intestinal bacteria and sometimes disease organisms that can make other campers sick.

Learn how to dispose of waste correctly. Dig a hole that is six to eight inches (fifteen to twenty centimeters) deep, where

Most campsites have specially designated receptacles for human waste and other garbage. Never leave your trash in the woods; take it with you when you leave!

decomposing microorganisms can thrive. Keep the sod lid intact and set it aside. Pile the rest of the dirt next to it. Then you're ready to do your business!

Afterward, scoop the dirt into the hole. Use a stick to mix the waste into the dirt. Replace the sod lid and camouflage the hole as much as possible. Don't bury used toilet paper. Always take it with you. You may have heard that to be ecologically kind you should use leaves instead of toilet paper. Don't. You might get an infection from dirty leaves or, even worse, poison ivy or poison oak.

Where do you dig a hole? You must keep a distance of at least two hundred feet (sixty-one meters) (about seventy paces) from natural water sources. Avoid places where your waste may be transported by flooding, runoff, or groundwater seepage. Keep your waste from being found by people and wildlife; keep a distance of two hundred feet (sixty meters) from campsites, trails, and food sources for animals, as well.

Some campers even carry their own portable latrines, available at outdoor suppliers. They empty the waste at approved dump sites. Never throw human waste in a trash can or dumpster, because this is also a health hazard and is illegal in most states. Park officials can tell you where such waste is collected.

Urinate in places where the urine can evaporate quickly, such as on rocks and in sunny areas. Stay at least two hundred feet (sixty-one meters) away from natural water sources.

RUB-A-DUB-DUB

After going to the bathroom in the woods, be sure to wash up. Don't risk getting sick by preparing food with contaminated hands. But how do you do this without contaminating the environment with your soapsuds? Soap has chemicals that can kill fish and plants. Leave soap at home, but use wet hand wipes from any grocery store. Remember, the fragrance-free kind won't attract bears and bees. You can also use waterless hand cleansers or hand sanitizers. Look for a brand that contains zinc pyrithione, an antimicrobial agent. Rub the cleanser on your hands, wipe off the excess, and you're clean.

As for your hair and body, you can wash them when you're back home. If you must do it outdoors, apply all the rules for

Be mindful of rivers and streams. They may be water supplies for humans or animals, so never pollute them with soap or human waste.

protecting water sources and keep your use of soap to a minimum. Never soap up and then jump in a stream to rinse off. Save the rinsing water and reuse it to clean your pots and pans. Try washing dishes with wet sand or coarse soil instead of soap. The sand works like a scouring pad, so food scrapes off easily.

BREAKING CAMP

If you have been organized and environmentally conscious while camping, it will make breaking camp easy. If you made a fire, make sure the fire pit is cold. Do not scatter leftover firewood

CONSERVATION EDUCATION

If you're passionate about conservation, the United States Department of Agriculture's Forest Service has all sorts of education programs to teach you about conservation. Conservation means appreciating and protecting our natural resources, including the plants, animals, and water sources that we find in nature. On the Forest Service's website (http://www.fs.usda.gov/) there is plenty of information on how you can keep your impact in the woods to a minimum. If you're passionate about conservation, contact your local US Forest Service and learn how you can get involved in nature and conservation!

among the trees. Make a neat stack next to the fire pit. Check for litter, which you will take with you, then cover the depression with fresh dirt or gravel.

Pick up all garbage around the camp, especially plastic or other non-biodegradable items. Do not leave behind any food, which may attract animals to the camp. Do not bury garbage; bears will find it and dig it up. If you burn garbage, you still have to take the unburned parts with you.

After taking down your tent, scatter natural debris over the ground where it stood. When your camp looks as if you were never there, then you're finished.

BIODEGRADABLE Something that can decompose or decay and be absorbed by the environment.

CONSERVATION The protection of natural resources such as trees, rivers, and minerals.

CRYPTOSPORIDIUM A parasite found in untreated water that causes fever, vomiting, fatigue, and diarrhea.

DECOMPOSE To rot or decay.

DEHYDRATION When the body, an organ, or a bodily part loses too much water.

FLAMMABLE Able to be set on fire easily.

GIARDIA A parasite found in untreated water that causes stomach cramps, diarrhea, and vomiting.

HEATSTROKE A serious illness caused by exposure to excessive heat.

HYPOTHERMIA A serious illness caused by exposure to excessive cold.

OUTFITTER A person or store that furnishes equipment for special purposes, such as camping.

PARASITE An animal or plant that lives on or in another animal or plant.

PARKA A warm fur or cloth jacket with a hood.

PITCH To set up, as in "to pitch a tent."

PROLONGED Occurring over a long period of time or consistently.

SYNTHETIC A material made by people that is not found in nature.

TARP A waterproof piece of material used to protect things from moisture; also called a tarpaulin.

TOURNIQUET A type of constrictive bandage used in the past (although now known to be ineffective) to control the spread of venom in the body.

VISTAS Wide, open views of a natural area, such as lakes or woods.

FOR MORE INFORMATION

American Camp Association (ACA)
5000 State Road 67 North
Martinsville, IN 46151
(800) 428-2267
Website: http://www.ACAcamps.org
ACA is an organization of camping professionals who dedicate their knowledge and experience to camping programs and youth development. They offer accreditation programs and resources for campers nationwide.

Canadian Forest Service (CFS)
580 Booth Street
Ottawa, ON
K1A 0E4
Canada
(800) 387-2000
Website: http://www.nrcan.gc.ca/forests
CFS is a part of Natural Resources Canada, the Canadian government's federal department that ensures the sustainability and maintenance of the forest sector throughout Canada. It conducts research and offers resources to the public on the forests of Canada.

Canadian Institute of Forestry (CIF)
P.O. Box 99
6905 Highway 17 West
Mattawa, ON POH 1V0
Canada
(705) 744-1715 ext. 609
Website: http://www.cif-ifc.org
Formed in 1908, the CIF is the voice of foresters, forest technologists, ecologists, educators, and countless others involved in the forestry industry. It promotes leadership in the industry and public awareness of forestry issues.

Canadian Parks and Wilderness Society (CPAWS)
506-250 City Centre Avenue
Ottawa, ON K1R 6K7
Canada
(800) 333-WILD
Website: http://www.cpaws.org
CPAWS is responsible for the creation of a vast amount of Canada's protected areas.
It works tirelessly to meet its goal: protecting over half the public land and water
throughout Canada.

National Park Service (NPS)
1849 C Street NW
Washington, DC 20240
(202) 208-6843
Website: http://www.nps.gov
The NPS is the US federal agency that oversees all US national parks. Its youth-ori-
ented programs promote conservation, ecology, and nature-friendly
attitudes for young people nationwide.

New York State Department of Environmental Conservation (DEC)
625 Broadway
Albany, NY 12233
(800) 456-CAMP
Website: http://www.dec.ny.gov
New York State's DEC is dedicated to preserving and protecting New York's natural
resources. It provides resources and information for campers and outdoor enthusi-
asts, including licenses and permits.

Sierra Club
85 Second Street, 2nd Floor
San Francisco, CA 94105
(415) 977-5500
Website: http://www.sierraclub.org

With sixty-four chapters nationwide and over 2.4 million members, the Sierra Club is one of the largest and most influential grassroots organizations dedicated to environmentalism in the United States.

USDA Forest Service
1400 Independence Avenue SW
Washington, DC 20250
(800) 832-1355
Website: www.fs.fed.us
The USDA Forest Service manages 154 national forests throughout the United States and Puerto Rico, with the goal of protecting and preserving US forests and grasslands for generations to come. They provide resources to young people and educators who are passionate about nature and conservation.

WEBSITES

Because of the changing nature of Internet links, Rosen Publishing has developed an online list of websites related to the subject of this book. This site is updated regularly. Please use this link to access this list:

http://www.rosenlinks.com/OUT/Camp

FOR FURTHER READING

Einspruch, Andrew. *Leaving a Light Footprint*. Mankato, MN: Smart Apple Media, 2011.

Emergency Preparedness. Irving, TX: Boy Scouts of America & American Red Cross, 2012.

Hardyman, Robyn. *Camping* (Adventures in the Great Outdoors). New York, NY: Windmill Books, 2014.

Honovich, Nancy, and Julie Beer. *Get Outside Guide: All Things Adventure, Exploration, and Fun!* Washington, D.C.: National Geographic, 2014

Jenson-Elliott, Cynthia L. *Camping* (Wild Outdoors). Mankato, MN: Capstone Press, 2011.

Lundgren, Julie K. *Camping* (Fun Sports for Fitness). Vero Beach, FL: Rourke Publishing Group, 2014.

Mason, Paul. *Hiking and Camping: The World's Top Hikes and Camping Spots*. Mankato, MN: Capstone Press, 2011.

Navarre, Gabrielle. *Cool Careers Without College for People who Love Nature*. New York, NY: Rosen Publishing, 2014.

Nickens, T. Edward. *Field & Stream's Guide to Outdoor Survival*. New York, NY: Gareth Stevens Publishing, 2015.

Richardson, Gillian. *Hiking* (Exploring the Outdoors). New York, NY: AV2 by Weigl, 2014.

Tomljanovic, Tatiana. *Camping* (Exploring the Outdoors). New York, NY: AV2 by Weigl, 2014.

York, M. J. *Camping* (Great Outdoors). Mankato, MN: The Child's World, 2015.

INDEX

V

Vibrio cholerae, 32

W

waste disposal, 51–53
water filters, 32, 33
water treatment, 31–33

ABOUT THE AUTHORS

Barry Mableton is a nature lover and camping aficionado. He lives in quaint Castleton-on-Hudson in Upstate New York.

Jacqueline Ching is a New York–based writer and editor.

PHOTO CREDITS

Designer: Brian Garvey; Editor: Jacob Steinberg

Photo researcher: Nicole Baker